MW00937324

ALWAYS PLAY
TO **WIN**

My father, Derek Jones, taught me so much growing up. His words are so empowering, they have definitely shaped me to be the woman I am today. I hope his quotes have the same impact on you as they do me. **- Madison Jones**

ALWAYS PLAY TO WIN

QUOTES BY

DEREK JONES

Project management by V E Harris Consulting Group, LLC
Book design and website by Beale Bagley Creations, LLC
Photographs by Duke University Photography
Back cover photo by Naketa Jones
Printed by Professional Printers, Columbia, S.C.

The Institute for Emerging Leaders, Incorporated, a 501 (c)3 organization will help facilitate projects to support programs with various charities and scholarships for students. Proceeds from #Ap2w will support these efforts.

This book is dedicated to my parents,

Thomas and Lucille Jones,

as a token of appreciation

for all the guidance, knowledge, and

wisdom they have given to me.

CONTENTS

FOREWORD

#Ap2w *Always Play to Win* – Great, godly wisdom for athletes, coaches, parents, and business executives...

Derek Jones has always been a winner on and off the field. As his high school principal in the early 1990's, I witnessed his positive and contagious spirit as he interacted with students, teachers, and his coaches at Woodruff High School. He was an individual State Track Champion in the 100 and 200-meter dashes and shared the State Championship Runners-Up title as a member of the 4 x 100 meter relay team. He was the Most Valuable Player (MVP) in track and field and football multiple years, as well as All-Conference defensive back in football. Derek is also a member of the Woodruff High School Athletic Hall of Fame. However, it was not his speed and agility that made him special. It was and is his relentless pursuit of excellence, and his willingness to persevere and maintain a winning attitude at all costs.

This "never quit" attitude led him to a successful collegiate career at the University of Mississippi and to a stellar career as a coach at the University of Mississippi, Murray State University, Middle Tennessee State University, University of Tulsa, University of Memphis, and then to where he currently serves as an assistant coach working with corner-backs for the highly respected Duke University Blue Devils.

#Ap2w

It is Derek's commitment to lifelong learning and commitment to others that have led him to share *#Ap2w, Always Play to Win.*

You will be blessed through his words of wisdom and encouragement. Derek epitomizes through his own life and example the development of character necessary to "win" in today's world.

His simple yet thoughtful approach in #Ap2w will provide a clear path for success. His contagious smile and positive spirit as portrayed in #Ap2w will challenge you to become the very best person you can be.

You will enjoy Derek's words of wisdom as they relate to people, relationships, priorities, faith, and even failures, just to name a few. He states, "Our vision, what we do and how we respond is the key to success." We MUST commit to a plan of action, or as Derek refers to it as "what we do."

I highly recommend #Ap2w Always Play to Win. Read it, embrace the message, and take action! Then, watch it change your life and the lives of those around you.

Dr. W. Rallie Liston
Spartanburg County School District Four Superintendent 2003-Present
Former Woodruff High School Principal 1989-2003
Milliken Foundation National Educator Award Winner 1995

#Ap2w

PREFACE

Always play to win has always been my motto. It means thinking ahead, making wise decisions, maintaining a positive outlook, making sacrifices, paying attention to detail, doing the little things right, leading by example, being a good listener, surrounding yourself with the right people, being conscious of your surroundings, watching what you say, not taking shortcuts, finishing what you start, being a person of your word, being humble, being a person of integrity, being reliable, being accountable, being responsible, protecting your reputation, having self respect, being respectful of others, being presentable, being professional, not afraid to be different, having drive, having determination, persevering, thinking before you act or react, being a good friend, family member, companion, and above all being a good spouse and parent. *Ap2w* is a way of life.

ACKNOWLEDGEMENTS

This book would not have been possible without the tireless effort and relentless commitment of all the individuals involved especially, Vareva Evans-Harris for leading this effort and Cathy Bagley for design and production. I am also thankful to Robyn Culbertson for leading our proof-reading and editing teams as well as Dan Beale for the web design digital presence.

I am grateful to the leadership teams and innovators at Apple, Inc. and Facebook, Inc. Literally, all of my quotes were typed on my iPhone, and my Facebook page provided the forum for me to begin sharing my quotes publicly on social media. I would never have time to sit down in front of a computer and write.

I am indebted to the thousands of Facebook friends that liked my quotes and posted comments about the impact of their relevance and motivation.

Finally, I thank my wife, Naketa, my parents, and my three daughters for their unwavering love and inspiration.

#Ap2w

INTRODUCTION

I've never seen myself as a writer, but I've always been a deep thinker. Several years ago, I decided to start writing my thoughts into quotes as a way to share them with others. At times they relate to certain situations and at times they are simply random thoughts I think others would like or need to hear. Much of what I've learned in life comes from my own personal experiences, but a lot stems from my observations of others as well. Life has a way of teaching lessons, whether through personal experience or through watching the experiences of others.

I was blessed as a child to have a great family structure, and both of my parents were huge influences in my life. I hear their voices even when they are not around, and I often wonder how they would respond to various situations before I react. I had an older brother who I could look up to and lean on for advice. I had great teachers and coaches who taught me lessons I still carry with me. I had family members, mentors and friends who have all helped mold me into the person I am today. Because of their influences on me, I want to be someone who impacts and has a lasting affect on the lives of others. I realize everyone may not have the support I was blessed to have; therefore if my words can fill a void or give advice I'm happy to provide that. I feel compelled as well as obligated to help others because of the many blessings I've had.

You can't control the things that happen to you in life, but how you react or respond to them is completely up to you.

As a man, I believe the ultimate goal in life is to be a good husband and a good father. I'm fortunate to be the father of 3 daughters and my obligation to each of them is to be a good friend as well. Far too many fathers shy away from certain conversations with their daughters because it makes them uncomfortable. There are certain things only a man can educate a woman on. I've always been very open and honest with each of my girls because it's my responsibility to teach them about the things the world is going to eventually expose them to. A lot my advice to them comes from my own personal experiences. I don't want the first time they hear or see something to be from someone who doesn't have their best interests at heart. I'm still able to think like a teenager because I've been a teenager, and I'm still able to think like a young adult because I've been a young adult. I understand a boy's way of thinking because I've been a boy, and I understand a man's way of thinking because I am a man. The messages to my daughters are for every female to see and understand. I realize these are hard lessons to learn without firsthand experience, but that's no excuse to not advise my children. I can't predict how a man will treat either of my daughters, but I never want them to be blindsided by something I should have brought to their attention. I want to have the same impact on them my parents had on me. I want them to always hear my voice saying, **"Always play to win!"**

Derek Jones

Photo by Duke University Photography

Everything you do in life is an interview because you never know who's watching or what they're looking for.

PEOPLE

People will tell you what you want to hear in order to get what they want. It's up to you to make them show you what you want to see before you give it to them.

When you allow other people's opinions to affect your way of thinking, doing things or behaving, you've lost control of who you truly are. Always stay true to yourself no matter what others think of who you are.

People can only use you if you allow them to. #Ap2w

If people are hating on you, don't let it faze you because you're probably doing something right. People don't usually hate on those who don't have much of anything going for them.

As hard as it may be, sometimes you have to make a decision to separate yourself from people who are holding you back in order to move forward.

If people are only drawn to you because of ability, appearance, status, titles, material things or money, what good are you to them when it fades, becomes outdated or disappears? Who you truly are is the most important thing you will ever be.

#Ap2w

People have a choice whether or not to believe your words, but they can never question your actions.

Being nice is a wonderful quality, but it's also an invitation for others to try and take advantage of you. People who are not like you will, with no conscience, try to drain you for every ounce of good in you if you allow them to. Never feel as if you owe people anything just because it's in your nature to give everything.

People will tell you that they have your best interest at heart when you have something they want or can benefit from. If they truly have your best interest at heart they shouldn't have to tell you.

People don't all of a sudden start acting a certain way. They generally just make the mistake of showing their true colors.

People will forever try to bring you down with negativity. Therefore lift yourself so high with positivity that you put yourself out of their reach. #Ap2w

Some people can get so caught up in looking for what's perfect that they become blind to what may be ideal. Happiness is just as much about the process as it is the product. You've gotta be willing to work, grow and sacrifice in order to benefit, gain and prosper.

#Ap2w

You should never have to wonder where you stand or if you really matter to someone. People don't neglect or abandon true priorities.

Some people will resent your strength because of their weakness.

Some things or people are not meant to be figured out. They are meant to be left alone. #Ap2w

No matter what connection you have, how long you've known them or what relation they are to you, people with agendas are not genuine because genuine people don't have agendas.

People will show you how much you mean to them without you having to ask. You've just got to decide if you truly want to see it or not.

People who constantly try to get over very rarely get ahead. There's no shortcut to success of any kind. It takes hard work, sacrifice and commitment to the process.

People can only take advantage of you if and for as long as you allow them to. There's a fine line between someone hurting or betraying you and you setting yourself up for disappointment, ignoring their intentions, giving them the benefit of the doubt or simply allowing it to happen.

#Ap2w

People with little or nothing to lose will often try to persuade or provoke you into doing something that could cause you to lose everything.

If people don't volunteer to tell you information, then they probably don't want you to know. Personal business starts with "personal" for a reason. #Ap2w

Don't put anything on social media that you may one day regret. You can delete it, but you can't take it back. Social media is not the place to vent or air your dirty laundry. Whether you're a mother, father, son, daughter, sister or brother, we all represent someone. When you express internet anger, people only see the image of you.

Your idea or definition of success will determine the type of people you attract. Genuineness and humility have a way of pulling people in while simultaneously shielding others away. The type of success you want depends on the type of people you want around you.

Very rarely do you see people who have it together worried about other people or their business. As odd as it seems, it's usually those who don't have it together who concern themselves with the business of others. If you make your business a full-time job, you won't have time to work anyone else's part-time job.

#Ap2w

People usually know when you're trying to take advantage of them. Some people will not confront you because they choose to keep down confusion. Others will let it be because of their character.

Beware of people who always seem to know and want to discuss everything about everyone else but themselves. If they're telling you other people's business, they're telling your business to other people.

People will intentionally try to cut you off, blindside or even run you off the road in life, but keep in mind that they can't do any of this if you leave them behind. Just stay in your lane and keep your foot on the gas.

Don't ever be mad at someone because they **choose not to** entertain drama, spread gossip, mind other people's business, act immature, carry themselves in a disrespectful manner or participate in activities that you have chosen.

People who live to impress others are rarely satisfied with themselves. #Ap2w

The people who are there for you when they're unaware of just how much you need them are the ones you want to keep around.

#Ap2w

T A L K

Oftentimes, saying nothing at all says enough. The more you argue with someone who doesn't know what they're talking about, the more you look as if you don't know what you're talking about.

Despite what we may think or assume should happen, everyone who reaches a certain age does not necessarily reach a certain level of maturity. There are tons of adults with sound minds who still talk, gossip, act and behave like teenagers or even kids despite their age. Maturity is a mind-set. It has no age limit.

Dramatic people hang around, talk to and gossip with other dramatic people. The rumors they instigate or entertain generally only circulate among their groups or other people just like them. If you are a drama-free person, the company you keep, people that are important or have an effect on you are probably just like you and that's really all that should matter.

Know when to talk and when to listen. Oftentimes people are not concerned with what you know as much as with what you're willing to learn.

You may call me confident, cocky, conceited and even arrogant by perception, but you will never be able to call me lazy, unmotivated, inconsistent or complacent by observation. Don't ever concern yourself with or be ashamed of anything you've sacrificed or worked hard to obtain.

If people are hating on you or are in your business, it's generally a result of jealousy. You have something they want or they wish they had. Let them be miserable as a result of it.

Don't ever try to talk someone else down to lift yourself up. Genuine people can sense when you're hating, and it generally makes you look bad instead of the person you're trying to tarnish the image of.

Don't ever try to talk someone else down to lift yourself up. #Ap2w

The higher you get the more people will be looking to bring you down. Very rarely do people gossip about, slander or spread rumors about irrelevant individuals. Your daily purpose should be to be the best you that you can be. Give your haters something to talk about, because it probably means you're something they're not or wish they were.

Exercise your right to vote! Regardless of what you believe, stand for or support, you don't stand for or support much of anything if you don't cast your vote. Regardless of how much you talk, your vote is the only voice you really have.

#Ap2w

RELATIONSHIP

A person who is not willing to change will always complicate growth in a relationship.

When it comes to relationships, the mistake is not initially choosing the wrong person because there's no way to know. The mistake is failing to realize, admit and accept that you've chosen the wrong person once you're involved.

When it comes to relationships, don't mistake bad luck for bad taste in those you choose.

It doesn't matter what obstacles you're faced with in a relationship as long as you're ready and willing to face them together. #Ap2w

People who don't have relationship issues generally don't concern themselves with the relationship issues of others. People who have relationship issues or no relationship at all commonly concern themselves with everybody else's issues except their own.

#Ap2w

RESPONSIBILITY

The more you depend on others to do things for you, the more you're generally going to be disappointed that they don't do things the way you want them done or they don't get them done at all.

Every time you leave it up to someone else to take care of your responsibilities, you're taking a gamble. No one is responsible for you but you. #Ap2w

A man should never expect credit for being a good husband or father. Once you take on either role, it's a responsibility, not a charity.

Don't ever allow someone who doesn't know you to have a false opinion of you that affects you in a negative way. It's not your responsibility to prove who you are to everyone observing you from afar.

It's pointless to pray for things you're not willing to work to obtain or maintain. If prayer opens the door, it's your responsibility to walk through it. Don't expect God to open the door and carry you as well.

PRIORITY

There's no such thing as too busy or not having time. If someone doesn't call, text, respond, reach out or make time for you, that's a pretty good indication of where you are on their priority list. People always find a way to make time for the things that are important to them.

As a parent, if being a parent isn't your top priority, you've got your priorities out of order.

In order for you to be the best that you can be for others, you have to make it a priority to set aside time to take care of yourself. #Ap2w

Don't ever allow someone to steal your thunder because they've lost their lightning. The only person in this world that you have complete control of is you; therefore, it's essential that you make it a priority to be good to yourself.

Don't ever take a woman out to eat at a restaurant that you can't afford, and beware of her if she frowns upon or refuses to eat at the places that you can afford.

#Ap2w

SUCCESS

There are people in your daily life who will cross or back-stab you in order to get something you have, prevent you from getting something they want or tarnish the image others have of you. It's caused by greed, jealousy, selfishness and often-times lust. The more of your personal business you disclose to them, the more of a target you will become. They will give you signs of their true character and intent by the questions they ask or how they behave towards you. You have to be wise enough to accept the fact that they're capable of betrayal.

You can't blame anyone but yourself for never accomplishing or achieving the things you never tried to accomplish or achieve. #Ap2w

The more you try to achieve, the more negative labels you are going to receive. It's sad but true that not everyone wants to see you prosper. If you lose people on your climb to success, it's a blessing because they never meant you much good anyway.

Don't make a habit of giving others the benefit of the doubt if you want to be successful at anything in life. Any organization that does its due diligence and makes indi-viduals earn their titles or positions has a better chance at success than one who makes assumptions or gives the benefit of the doubt. Relationships are no exception.

#Ap2w

No matter what you do, who you surround yourself with is a key element to success. Very rarely will you progress if the person or people around or closest to you are content standing still.

Never put a price tag on happiness or success. Instead base your happiness on peace of mind. There are people with great jobs, impressive salaries, nice homes and what appears to be the ideal life on the surface who are stressed, lonely, unhappy and depressed because they lack the simple things in life that are free.

If you're constantly trying to make things work instead of allowing things to work, you're generally dealing with the wrong people. Relationships of any kind take work, but they're not supposed feel like a stressful full-time job.

Generosity is often rewarded, whereas selfishness rarely reaps many benefits. #Ap2w

If you constantly surround yourself with people who stress, frustrate or bring you down, you're constantly going to be stressed, frustrated and down.

In order to find peace of mind you have to rid yourself of people who are constant distractions or burdens and who cause you pain and stress. No matter what relation they are to you, how long you've been together or associated, some people are simply not good or healthy for you.

#Ap2w

A simple formula for success: Don't be afraid to fail. Prepare to deal with failure. Learn from failure, and have a plan to rebound from failure. Refuse to accept failure.

UNDERSTAND

Lack of communication leads to misconception and misunderstanding, which leads to damaged or ruined relationships. Never be too prideful to be the bigger person and understand not to take the little things for granted.

People who don't know you will label you only because they can't relate to or understand you. #Ap2w

It's hard for someone who's not a genuine and sincere person to understand genuine and sincere acts by others. They will generally think there's a motive to your acts of kindness because they generally have a motive to their acts of kindness.

BETTER

You should never have to ask or plead for someone to be nice to you or treat you right. If you do, understand that you deserve better. People can only treat you how you allow them to treat you.

#Ap2w

Just because I don't talk to you doesn't mean I think I'm better than you. It simply means I don't want to be associated with you because of how you act, carry yourself and the things you say and do.

Don't make a lot of false resolutions. Just strive to be better today than you were yesterday and better tomorrow than you will be today.

I don't think I'm any better than you. I'm simply on a mission to be the best me that I can be. #Ap2w

I'm in the percentage of college football players who got into an NFL camp but didn't make it in the NFL. I'm also in the percentage that didn't depend on making it in the NFL. My father told me from the time I was in grade school through high school through college, "Boy, you better get your books! Education gives you far more options than athletics."

If you don't feel as if you've changed for the better in the past year, month or even week, you need to evaluate what you're doing for personal growth.

I learned at a young age to ignore those who didn't like me, to overlook those who talked or looked down on me, to be kind to those who were mean to me, to be thankful for those who rejected me, to welcome those who doubted me and to pray for those who didn't believe in me because it all made me better. You can either be agitated by negativity or motivated by it. It's all in your attitude.

Don't ever allow someone's perception of you to hold you back from trying to elevate yourself.

You can't go back and do the things you should have done, so you better do them right now.

L I F E

Life is too short to live worrying about how people view you or what they will say about you because you do something that they've never had the guts to do. Trying to live politically correct in the eyes of others lessens the potential thrills of life. It's okay to step outside of the box from time to time. Life is about living.

Always be prepared to encounter and endure adversity. Life doesn't always provide warning signs. #Ap2w

People are always looking for something to talk or gossip about, whether they have facts to support their information or not. If you allow things people say about you to worry you, you'll be stressed for life. Just ignore nonsense and keep it moving.

#Ap2w

Be careful who you seek or accept advice from. Some people are simply in no position to tell you what you should do about your life's issues because they have no handle on or control over their own.

When people show you who they really are, don't try to diagnose yourself with amnesia because you want or think you need them in your life. See it for what it's worth and keep them at a distance or move on. You will be much better off in the long run.

You can sit around for the rest of your life wondering what you could have been or you can make up your mind to live your life and become what you should be. #Ap2w

People who get offended by the things you post or assume you are talking about them usually have a reason to assume so. Guilt triggers curiosity. Life is pretty simple. If the shoe fits, wear it. If it doesn't fit, place it back on the shelf and keep moving. There should be no reason to wonder.

Don't ever wish you had someone else's life, because you have no idea what's genuine about it and what isn't. People only showcase what they want others to see and very rarely will they reveal the things they don't want others to see. Instead of wishing for someone else's life, focus on making the most of your own.

#Ap2w

A big part of maturity is outgrowing people, places and things. Don't ever feel as if you have to revisit your past in order to fit in. Some people, places and things in life are simply meant to be memories.

Whether you like it or not people will label you based on appearance and not because of who you are. Treat everything you do in life like an interview because you never know who's watching or what they're looking for.

MOMENT

The best way to keep someone's interest is to remain interesting. Whether you're a male or female, the moment you become complacent is the moment someone else becomes appealing. Regardless of what you've done in the past, what you've provided or how much you've invested, every day is a new day when it comes to relationships. Regardless of how long you've been together, always remember people like what they fell for, not necessarily what you've become. If you're no longer doing or providing those moments, smiles or memories, you're not fulfilling their wants, needs or desires.

We are measured and remembered in life by what we do or how we perform in our most defining moments. #Ap2w

#Ap2w

The moment you stoop to the level of those who betray, take advantage of or slander you is the moment you put yourself in the same category as them. Words or acts against you should never change who you truly are.

Make the most of your time, appreciate your moments and make memories. One day you will dearly miss someone you have the chance to do each of these things with regularly. Allow people to smell your flowers, see your smile, read your poems or hear your kind words while they are alive and well.

Make the most of your time, appreciate your moments and make memories. #Ap2w

The moment you react or respond to haters, critics, gossipers or liars is the moment you allow them to become relevant. If a person has that much time to mind your business, they probably don't have much of their own. A fire will eventually burn out without anything to fuel it.

You can't control people's actions towards you but you can control your reactions to them. The higher you get the more people will try to pull you down with lies, deceit, rumors, jealousy and betrayal, but your maturity level should always keep you out of their reach. The moment you react to them is the moment you categorize yourself with them.

#Ap2w

PROGRESS

Worrying about yesterday will only restrict or prevent you from progressing today. Getting knocked down is a part of life. Lying down is a choice.

It's sad but true that some of the closest people to you are the ones you need to distance yourself the farthest from in order to progress.

You can only carry dead weight so far before it starts to slow or pull you down. As hard as it may be sometimes you have to cut people loose in order stay afloat or progress.

Getting knocked down is a part of life. Lying down is a choice. #Ap2w

Sometimes you have to walk away from people, places or things that have been in your life for all or most of it in order to progress.

#Ap2w

H A P P Y

One of the greatest joys in life is **not** having the burden of worrying about what others think of you. You can't please everyone, and no matter how hard you try to get along, some people are just messy, jealous and opposed to seeing others happy. As long as you are happy or content with the reflection that you see in the mirror, don't worry about the image that others see.

One of the hardest lessons in life to learn – but one that we all must learn – is that you can't please or make everyone around you happy.

You must be happy with yourself in order to make someone else happy. #Ap2w

You can't go through life worrying about everyone else's opinion of you. It's a fact of life that you will never be able to please or make everyone around you happy, and everyone around you or in your circle does not necessarily want you to be happy. Jealousy is a disease that affects millions, but it doesn't mean it has to affect you.

One of the hardest lessons to learn in life is no matter how hard you try you are not capable of making everyone in your life happy. Someone is always going to want more, and you will constantly fall short in the eyes of others. Stay true to yourself.

#Ap2w

You don't owe anyone an apology for doing things to make yourself happy. People will try to rain on your parade because of their own personal storms. If they can't simply be happy for you, then their opinions should be irrelevant to you.

It doesn't cost a fortune to make someone happy or put a smile on their face. It simply costs a little time, effort and creativity.

Some people say they can't afford to be happy. I can't afford to be unhappy. The days of my life are too valuable to waste on sadness, stress or uncertainty. #Ap2w

Strive for self-approval not public approval. No matter how hard you try, you will never be able to please everyone who is critical of you. If you spend your time trying to do so you are simply wasting your time. You have to be happy with the reflection you see in the mirror before you concern yourself with the image others see from afar.

Gossip usually rotates in circles of similar minded people. They either don't have business of their own or they're unhappy with the business they have.

Don't ever question who or what makes you happy. Over-analyzing the obvious only takes away from good times, happiness or fond memories you could be making. Life is about living.

#Ap2w

SITUATION

None of us can turn back the hands of time to change our past, but we all have the ability to determine our future. No matter what your current situation is, every day is an opportunity to better yourself. It all depends on how much you truly want to change or better yourself.

Never worry or concern yourself with those who talk negatively about, label or pass judgment on you without having first-hand knowledge of your situation because they're generally the ones who have little or no room to do any of the above.

You can't continue to do the things that put you in bad situations or predicaments and expect to progress. #Ap2w

If you don't see the good in a situation you will be blinded by the bad. It's all in your attitude.

Every relationship deserves its own due process. Comparing one situation to another only stalls or limits the possibility of growth.

#Ap2w

ENERGY

Holding a grudge is a waste of energy because it generally affects you far more than it affects the person you are holding it against. Instead of being mad or upset, if you know what they are about just take the person in small doses or distance yourself from them all together.

**Stop wasting time making excuses
and focus your energy
toward finding solutions.** #Ap2w

It takes too much energy to dislike or hate anyone. It's much easier to just ignore them all together.

Don't waste your time worrying about things you can't control. Life is too short to try and move things that can't be moved, change things that you cannot change or affect things you have no effect on. Spend your time and energy where you can actually make a difference. It's a lot less stressful.

Don't waste your time, effort or energy trying to impress those who have no effect on your daily existence or progress.

Don't give your doubters, haters or enemies the satisfaction of allowing their words, looks or actions to bring you down.

#Ap2w

It takes enough time and energy to entertain those who you're in good graces with; there's not enough to waste on those who are on your bad side or on the outside looking in. No response is the best response.

Don't worry about things you can't control. Focus your time and energy on things you can actually affect or change.

P R O B L E M

It's okay to admire others, but never wish you had someone else's life. You have no idea what problems or issues they have beyond what you see on the surface. Everything that seems or looks good is not always peaches and cream.

It's generally not an accident that the same people repeatedly have the same problems. We are all products of the situations that we put ourselves in. #Ap2w

Thinking too much or over analyzing can often cause you to rethink, doubt or second guess what you know, what's been proven or is untarnished. Don't ever allow outside influences or personal insecurities to cause or create problems that don't exist.

It's a common thing for others to feel entitled to or expect benefits from your hard work, sacrifice and dedication.

#Ap2w

They constantly take and never give. They always have an excuse or story as to why they constantly have the same set of problems, and they have a way of trying to make you feel as if you owe them something. A user will use you up as long as you allow them to, and when they have sucked you dry they simply move on to someone else without shame, regret or remorse.

Impatience will cause or contribute to far more problems than it solves. #Ap2w

No matter how bad things are for you, how extreme your problems may be or how hard it may be to deal with them, every day something happens that makes someone else think the same thing about themselves and their life. Someone always has it just as bad as or worse than you.

Who would you turn to and know you could depend on if you had a problem tomorrow? Don't neglect to acknowledge and show appreciation to that person or those people today. Dependability, loyalty and security are rare characteristics in relationships of any kind that should never be taken for granted.

Personal problems are generally the result of personal actions or lack of them. Who we deal with, depend on, listen to, spend time with, follow, are influenced by, or chose to be in a relationship with are all personal choices. As hard or painful as it may be, sometimes it takes change in order to progress. If you don't like what you're getting, change what you're doing.

Everyone needs to diet for their health from time to time, and I'm not referring to weight loss. I'm referring to the excess of people in your life who cause you stress, problems or who are simply not good or healthy for you. You can be so heavy it weighs you down and burdens you to the point of mental obesity. If a person constantly causes you stress, wants something from you, and is of no benefit, you need to rid yourself of them. No matter who they are or what role they may play in your life, sometimes you have to trim the fat in order to feel good about yourself.

If you don't like what you're getting, change what you're doing. #Ap2w

It's not about what the house looks like on the outside. It's about whether or not it feels like a happy home on the inside. People often look at the lives of others and wish they had their lives or situations because it appears they have it all together when in reality they have just as many or more problems and struggles. You have no idea how battered mentally or physically a pretty woman is, how much in debt a pro athlete or celebrity is, how stressed a politician or pastor is, how close to being broke a rich man is or how close to divorce the perfect couple is. Focus your time and energy on making your own life as good as it can be and refrain from wishing for the lives of others.

#Ap2w

You lesson your burdens by surrounding yourself with individuals who you don't have to always carry. When the people around you always have problems, they eventually become your problems.

It's not an accident that the same people tend to cause or have the same problems. If you are haunted by the same issues in life, take a good look at your habits because they are a direct reflection of your character.

A P O L O G I Z E

It's not your job to make everyone else happy, and you're not obligated to explain or apologize for being happy yourself. There's absolutely no harm in loving yourself and being proud of who you are.

Life is about moving forward... #Ap2w

Just because others won't let your past go doesn't mean you have to hold on to it. As long as you learned from it and you're a better person as a result of it, you no longer have to apologize for it. Life is about moving forward not looking backward.

People, who hurt, slander or betray you may apologize, but very rarely are they truly sorry. Most of the time they're just sorry that they got caught or you figured them out.

#Ap2w

DIFFERENT

A tree has to shed leaves in order to grow. People are no different. We have to shed behavior, habits and even people in order to move forward.

Sometimes we just grow in different directions. #Ap2w

Even though you may have been traveling together for all or most of your life, sometimes you have to take a different exit from people in your life in order to get to where you want to go.

Never apologize or feel bad because you don't do things that people around you do, go places that they like to go or behave and carry on the way they like to behave and carry on. It doesn't mean that you think you're any better than them. It simply means you're on a different page and that's okay.

Separating yourself doesn't mean you think you're any better than others. It simply means your priorities are different than theirs.

Very rarely are you truly blindsided by those individuals who betray, hurt or let you down. Ignoring their signs generally means that you're not ready or willing to face reality. Closing your eyes is different than being blind.

#Ap2w

Don't ever feel as if you have to look back to move forward. Most of the things and people you've left behind don't fit into your current situation. You don't have to relive your past, revisit former relationships or revert to old habits to coexist with those you've migrated from. Sometimes we just grow in different directions.

Don't ever be reluctant, afraid or ashamed to be different. Nothing would be unique about you if you were like everyone else. #Ap2w

When you look in the mirror the reflection you see is of you. No matter how many skin flaws or teeth imperfections, it's still you. Despite how much hair you have or used to have, it's still you. Regardless of how short or tall you are or what you weigh or don't weigh, it's still you. In spite of cosmetics, eyelashes, hair extensions or weave, it's still you. No matter how rough you've had it or how good you have it, it's still you. Regardless of your past or recent history, it's still you. You may not like what you see or wish it looked different, but it's still always going to be you. Therefore, if you don't already, learn to love you.

You will always come up short trying to be who or what someone else wants or needs you to be. If who you are isn't good enough for them, you should give your attention to someone who feels and thinks differently.

#Ap2w

Being different is not about thinking you're above anyone else, better than anyone else or on a different level than anyone else. It's about not being comparable to anyone else. Do things that others neglect to do, see things that others don't think to look for, hear things that others are talking too much to hear, recognize things that others aren't aware of, say things that others are too prideful to say, observe things that others are so busy they overlook, take your time when others are in a hurry and pay attention to detail when others fail to pay attention at all. Live to be different because different is rare.

FAMILY

My mom told me when I was young that my mouth would lead me to success one day if I ever figured out when to talk and when to be quiet. Everyone, regardless of age, should take my mom's advice. It still applies today, and I'm still listening to her words.

Family does not always have to be blood related. It simply has to be real. #Ap2w

Growing up, we played basketball at my grandmother's every Sunday. We had a dirt court with wooden poles, backboards and torn nets until my Aunt Frances decided to build us a cement court with steel breakaway backboards and chain nets. I'm sure it cost her a pretty penny, but she did it because she wanted us to have something to keep us focused and off of the streets. She once drove to our house to bring me some bananas after I had cramps in a high school football game. She supported my sports career as if I were her own son until she passed away in December 1992. As I look back, it makes me realize how fortunate we were as kids to have such a loving and supportive family and how amazing it is that this love still lives today.

Don't ever take family for granted. #Ap2w

Whether it's immediate or distant, there's nothing in the world like family. I'm blessed to have relatives close and abroad that act as influences on me in both my personal and professional life. We may not talk or speak every day, week or month, but knowing you have a support system is a daily source of strength and motivation. Family does not always have to be blood related. It simply has to be real.

A person who waits for bad things to happen and negatively tries to disrupt the chemistry of an organization, team, relationship or family is a virus. The best way to deal with them is to simply ignore them.

Take a little time to take care of yourself. We often get so caught up in work, daily routines, family responsibilities or doing for others that we neglect to cater to ourselves. No one knows how or what it takes to take care of you better than you, so take the time to do so.

#Ap2w

Everyone has the answers until people are pointing the fingers or asking the questions about you or someone you love. If your sentence starts with "They said," don't say it. If someone says to you "I heard," don't listen. Gossip is a common source of lack of progress in any relationship, organization, community or family.

STRONG

No matter how difficult or extreme it may have seemed at the time, when you think back on your past struggles in life not many of them affect you at this moment. We all have had problems that range from relationships, to finances, to emotional issues, to legal troubles, but through prayer, maturity and growth we've overcome them. Time generally heals all of life's non-health-related wounds. You just have to be strong enough to endure the pain.

You can either make an excuse or you can find a way. It's all in your attitude. #Ap2w

I may not always have been as talented as my competition, but I made it a point to be more disciplined. I may not have been as smart, but I made it a point to be more creative. I may not have had as much, but I made a point to make the most of what I had. I may not have been as big or strong, but I made it a point to be in better shape. Don't ever settle.

#Ap2w

You never realize how strong someone is until you've seen them rebound from their weakest moment.

People who appear to be weak are some of the strongest individuals you will encounter, while people who appear to be strong are often the weakest. The wilting tree has withstood the test of time. The tree that stands tall has yet to endure many hardships.

**Burdens can either wear you down
or make you stronger.
It's all in your attitude.** #Ap2w

The moment you react or respond to an idiot is the moment you place yourself in the same category as them. No matter how strong you may feel about something, sometimes saying nothing at all says enough. You will never go wrong being the bigger person.

Be careful who you hang around or associate yourself with because growth, or lack of it, is strongly affected by the company you keep. Sometimes you must drop dead weight in order to climb higher.

#Ap2w

HELP

We control most of our peace of mind. People will try to take advantage of you as long as you allow them. They will leave you to worry about their issues or problems as if you don't have your own and get upset with you for not helping to solve them. Saying no may seem hard, but it's really very simple.

The only time that you should look down on someone else is when you are reaching down and lending a helping hand to lift them up. #Ap2w

If it doesn't bother a person to ask you for a ridiculous favor, it shouldn't bother you to say no. People will use you as long as you allow them to and never once offer a helping hand to you.

We generally excel at the things we make our priorities and apply ourselves to. Some of those things help us to prosper, and sadly some of those things hinder us from prospering. If you take a look in the mirror, the image will probably reflect what you do or don't put your time into.

Today let everyone reflect on how far we've come, but not take for granted how far we still have to go. Disrespect and lack of equality is wrong, regardless of what race you are.

Some things in life are simply not worthy of entertaining or commenting on. You only help to spread the word of ignorant people when you repeat, discuss or comment publicly on the things they say.

The only thing you do when you attack someone's character is cause others to question your own character. Very rarely will hating on someone help you to get ahead.

Know who you can tell your problems to and who you can depend on to help solve them. No matter how well or how long you've known them, people with agendas will never have anyone's best interest at heart but their own.

Everyone around you is not necessarily healthy for you. Separating yourself from the wrong people will generally help you stay on the right track. #Ap2w

Being good to others shouldn't come at the expense of being broke, in a bind or miserable yourself. If every encounter between you and someone causes you misery or costs you time, effort or money, you need to reevaluate the relationship. Helping others here and there doesn't mean they should be dependent on you or that you're responsible for them.

#Ap2w

You can't consume yourself with trying to help someone who doesn't do much to help himself. If you're constantly bending over backwards to lend a helping hand and the person you're helping is doing nothing to pick himself up, it will eventually wear you down.

One of the hardest but most essential lessons to learn in life is that it's not your responsibility to solve other people's problems. Lending a helping hand is a choice, not an obligation.

VALUE

Don't ever allow anyone else to determine your worth. Always place value in yourself and refuse to settle for any less than you feel you deserve.

Just because someone doesn't recognize or appreciate your value doesn't mean it diminishes your worth. #Ap2w

For most of my young life I wanted to get to a point where I could afford anything I wanted. Then somewhere along the way, I realized there wasn't much I wanted that I didn't already have. My father demonstrated to me long ago that a good man works hard for most of his life so that those he's responsible for can be happy, live comfortably and have peace of mind. I just didn't realize this until I became a man. If you place your value and worth in material things, you will forever be a prisoner of what you want or don't have and blind to the things that you do have.

In a world where people place so much value on material things and assets, never lose sight of the fact that the most valuable assets you have are the things you would never give away, put a price tag on or sell. Treat them as such.

POSITIVE

Nothing positive generally comes from reacting or making decisions while upset or angry.

A mature person should never entertain immaturity, a positive person should never respond to negativity, and a secure person should never be affected by insecurity.

Looking back only keeps you from moving forward. If you can't let go of the negatives from your past, you will struggle to have a positive future.

Never stop thinking of ways to separate yourself from the norm in a positive manner. Anyone can be average. #Ap2w

You're probably not going to have a positive day if you have a negative attitude.

#Ap2w

Being a coach, I've come to realize that no matter how bad you may feel after a loss, nothing positive comes from being negative. It only generates more personal frustration and stress. Wondering "What if?" has never and will never change an outcome. When I want to feel better about anything I simply count my blessings.

Don't question those who are loyal, devoted or good to you because of those who are not. Value the good people in your life because you will only be blessed with a few.

EXPOSE

Everyone wants to come to your pool party. A lot of them will come to the ledge to see if you're okay when you fall in the water. Some of them will be willing to throw you a rope to try to save you. Not many will take the risk of stretching their arm out to help you. Less than that will make the sacrifice of jumping in the water to try to save you, and only a few will do whatever it takes to see that you don't drown. Tough times will always expose pretenders and fake people in your life and reveal real ones.

Unless you're without skeletons in your closet, don't speculate, gossip or try to expose the skeletons of others. #Ap2w

#Ap2w

I've done a lot of things in life that I'm not proud of, a lot of things I wouldn't want the public to know about, a lot of things I wouldn't want my mother to know about and a lot of things I wouldn't want my kids to duplicate. Therefore, I never judge someone else for the things they do or have done that get exposed. My mother always told me, "You don't have a heaven or hell to place someone, so pray for them instead of judging them."

Tough times will always expose pretenders and fake people in your life and reveal real ones. #Ap2w

Unless you're without skeletons in your closet, don't speculate, gossip or try to expose the skeletons of others. Keep in mind that there's always someone who knows what you've done, where you did it and who you did it with that could easily expose you.

Fake people in your life will expose themselves repeatedly. It's up to you whether you truly want to see what they are revealing.

Don't ever be upset when people expose their true character to you. As shocking, hurtful or disappointing as it may be, think of all the time, effort and energy it saves you long term. Everyone you invest in simply isn't going to have the same heart as you, and that's okay. We all live and learn.

#Ap2w

L O V E

Some people will dislike you for the same reasons that others love you. We were not created to please everyone, so don't worry yourself with trying. Just be you.

Learn to love and take care of yourself before you become dependent on others to do so. #Ap2w

When people hate, lie about, try to belittle or tarnish the image of someone else, it's often the result of jealousy, wanting something they have, wishing they were in the same position or personally feeling as if they are not on the same level. Jealousy is as bad as any disease you can have because it causes you suffering, unhappiness, misery, stress, insecurity and so much more. Worst of all, you have to live with it. If you truly love yourself, there's no reason to hate anyone else.

Take time to talk to the people you love while you still can. #Ap2w

Don't ever let someone cause you to second guess someone or something you truly believe in. People who lack passion in their lives will quickly drag you to their level if you allow them. Misery not only loves company, it also craves it!

#Ap2w

People will try to distract, slow down or stop you from progressing because they have no will to progress themselves. Happiness causes jealousy and misery. And jealousy and misery love company.

The more you depend on someone else or others to make you happy, the more power you give them to disappoint or let you down. Learn to love and take care of yourself before you become dependent on others to do so.

In order to be happy and keep a positive frame of mind, avoid surrounding yourself with negative people, listening to people's negativity and entertaining negative rumors or gossip. Just because misery loves company doesn't mean you have to be a visitor.

Jealousy is as bad as any disease you can have because it causes you suffering, unhappiness, misery, stress, insecurity and so much more. Worst of all, you have to live with it. If you, truly love yourself there's no reason to hate anyone else. #Ap2w

If you're on social media or have a cell phone to text, it takes less time to tell someone you love them than it takes to type an excuse why you can't or haven't.

#Ap2w

CHERISH

Some people spend their entire lives settling for what's acceptable in the eyes of others or convenient and never get the joy of what it truly feels like to be spontaneous, have fun or experience happiness. Grab a hold of, hold on to, go out to enjoy and cherish anything or anyone that has the power to give you butterflies in life, because life is too short not to live.

Cherish every moment that you have with the ones you love and understand that every day you have with them is a blessing. #Ap2w

Cherish the people who don't cause you stress and distance yourself from those who consume your peace of mind. Energy vampires will drain the joy and life out of you if you allow them to, and when they've bottomed you out they'll move on to someone else.

Regardless of the nature of the relationship, if you have something real when it comes to the people in your life you should appreciate and cherish it because it's very rare.

Cherish anyone who has the power make you smile without saying a word.

#Ap2w

ATTENTION

Some people in your life can and will handicap your growth if you give them too much of your time and attention.

When you do things from your heart with no agenda, there's no attention, recognition or even gratitude expected in return. You're simply being who you are.

Your present deserves the most attention, and you better pay more attention to your future than your past. A person who dwells on or lives in the past only limits their present or future. Life goes on, so keep it moving.

If we all paid more attention to our own business and affairs, life would be a lot less stressful.

Always pay attention to the people who matter in your life. #Ap2w

Message to boys and men: It generally does you no good to try and belittle, slander or hate on another man to get the attention of a woman or draw her attention away from him. Generally, all you do by talking negatively about him is heighten her curiosity about him. It's simply not a good look for a man of any age at any time.

What you don't pay attention to can't affect you.

#Ap2w

Devote your time and energy to things that you can actually influence or control and allow others to take care of the things that you can't. Life is stressful enough as it is, so why take on added burdens that have nothing to do with you?

Always pay attention to the people who matter in your life. Neglecting to do this will cause you to lose some of the most loyal and devoted people you will ever have in your corner.

A good way to avoid being disappointed is to pay less attention to what people tell you and more attention to the things they show you. #Ap2w

No matter what you can afford to financially give to those you love, always understand that the most valuable assets you have to share are time and attention.

If you have to ask someone for time, attention and affection now, you will probably have to beg for it later. Things like that usually get worse, not better.

Pay attention to detail and make a habit of doing little things better than those you're being compared to or are in competition with.

#Ap2w

MISTAKES

Lack of discipline is the source of most of our mistakes and regrets.

You shouldn't be making the same excuses or mistakes at 25 that you made at 15, at 35 that you made at 25, at 45 that you made at 35 and so on. If you are, you're simply treading water and should reevaluate what you truly want out of life. Making excuses will not change circumstances.

Never be embarrassed or ashamed of your past. Mistakes help to define who we are and structure who we will become. As long as you learn from them, embrace your mistakes as life lessons. #Ap2w

If you constantly apologize for making the same mistakes, people eventually stop believing that you're sorry or remorseful for making them.

There's no way to see the sincerity, beauty or good in someone unless you are willing to take the time to experience and explore them with an open mind and heart. You must allow anyone new who enters your life with good intentions and a clean slate to make their own mistakes. Comparing them to others in your past could prevent you from having a wonderful future.

One of the worst mistakes you can make is to try and make everyone around you happy or try to be what they want or expect you to be.

F A I T H

There are times in life that test our faith, and the only way for us to endure is to have faith.

No matter how hard or how many days it rains, the sun will eventually shine again. You just need to have the faith to weather the storm.

Faith is an all-the-time thing. #Ap2w

The only thing that you should question when you face death is your faith.

You can't call on God when things are bad if you don't show him gratitude when things are good. Faith is an all-the-time thing.

The less faith you have the harder it is to deal with the misfortunes, trials and tribulations of life. #Ap2w

Oftentimes we allow life to hold us hostage or prisoner because we don't want or know how to accept change. We all want to see results when we've invested in something, but sometimes we have to cut our losses to truly recognize our gains. Enduring pain makes us all stronger, but carrying dead weight or holding on to false hope will eventually wear the strongest person down. Place your time and faith in things that will eventually yield positive results. Rarely are we blind to reality; we just refuse to open our eyes and see it. Sometimes when we think we have to break the chain, all we really have to do is use our key.

FAILURE

Failure is not always about lack of talent. Oftentimes it's more about order of priority. If you simply do the things you have to do before you do the things you want to do, then you will generally give yourself a chance to be successful.

Don't get so caught up in multitasking that you fail to prioritize. Some things simply require and/or deserve more attention than others.

#Ap2w

Failure is a part of life, but it doesn't have to be a way of life. I never knew exactly what I wanted to be or was going to become, but I've always known what I wasn't going to be or allow myself to become.

I'm not ashamed of my mistakes, shortcomings or failures in life because they have been my most important source of education. A lot of those mistakes were made at an adult age, but not with an adult maturity level. A lot of the short-comings came as a result of trying to take short cuts and a lot of the failures came as a result of not being prepared to succeed.

I'm not ashamed of my mistakes, shortcomings or failures in life because they have been my most important source of education. #Ap2w

We all have to go through things in order to learn from our experiences. Despite how it may appear on the surface, I'm definitely no exception.

I've come up short just as many times as I've succeeded, but I've never become frustrated because my failures have always been my source of motivation to succeed.

Never take for granted or fail to take advantage of your opportunities. An opportunity you *have* today could be an opportunity you *had* tomorrow.

#Ap2w

We all fall or get knocked down at one time or another. Some of us choose to feel sorry for ourselves and lay down, while others refuse to accept failure or defeat and get back up. Failure is not about situations; it's about whether or not you accept them.

Always stay hungry. Complacency is the first step to failure. #Ap2w

You will never have peace of mind worrying yourself about other people's negative opinion of you. There's always going to be someone who dislikes you, doesn't agree with you or wants to see you fail. Let the negative energy affect them, not you.

Living in fear only keeps you from progressing. In order to move forward and work toward a brighter future, you have to release your failures, shortcomings, bad experiences or darkness from the past.

It's better to have failures of things you attempted on your personal resume than regrets of things you never tried.

#Ap2w

No matter how much time, energy and effort you put into someone or something that fails, don't view it as time wasted. Look at it as a lesson learned. Whether we've grown from them or we're still treading water, we are a product of our mistakes.

No matter how many times you come up short, you haven't failed until you've given up. #Ap2w

You can view your mistakes as either learning experiences or failures. It's all in your attitude.

I don't regret my failures, and I refuse to regret the things I never tried. Life is about living. I don't remember my last life so I choose to live this one.

TRUST

You can put so much stock into someone *else* making you happy that you easily neglect all of the things that have always made you happy. The only person that you can truly trust with your happiness and well-being is *you*, so never lose sight of what it takes to take care of you.

Trust those who don't make a lot of promises, but have a track record with you of simply being trustworthy without expecting anything in return.

There are times when you don't know exactly which way to go, what your next step is or what's behind the door in front of you, but rarely are there times when you don't have an idea. God never allows us to walk alone. We just have to believe that He's there. Trust your instincts. They will rarely lie to you.

You don't have to shower someone with material things in order to grasp or hold their attention. Time, smiles, sacrifice, communication, good conversation, trust, honesty and flattery are free.

Trust your instincts. They will rarely lie to you. #Ap2w

Be careful giving trust to anyone who hasn't earned it. Unfortunately, we live in a world where a large majority of the people we encounter wear masks that hide their true identities or intentions. If you're not careful, salt can easily be mistaken for sugar.

If you are sincere, people will be sincere with you. If you constantly try to play or get over on people, they will struggle to take you seriously because they can't trust you.

There is a fine line between giving someone the benefit of the doubt and giving someone your trust. If you give them the benefit of the doubt, they simply didn't pass your test. You shouldn't be hurt or disappointed. If you give them your trust before they pass the benefit of the doubt test, you are setting yourself up for hurt and disappointment. A lot of life's mistakes can be prevented if you set and hold others to your standards.

Always keep in mind that, regardless of the circumstances, one of the hardest things to do in life is to regain or re- establish trust after you've said or done something to lose or betray it. Think of the consequences before you act or speak.

Be careful giving trust to anyone who hasn't earned it. #Ap2w

Hyenas will do whatever it takes to survive and could care less who they strong-arm, manipulate or deceive in the process. They run in packs to get what they want, but each of them always has an individual agenda. They can't be trusted by members of their own pack, much less any other animal around them. Some individuals and groups of people are just like hyenas. They always have a personal agenda and could care less who they hurt, betray or back-stab in the process. If you know a person or circle consists of hyenas, stay away from them. No matter how cool, welcoming or nice they may seem, they're very dangerous at all times.

No matter how they may come across or appear on the surface, everyone you meet or have around you is not worthy of being in your circle. Problems generally arise and escalate because there are too many random people in what should be a close or tight knit circle. You can't control jealousy, rumors or gossip, but you can limit betrayal, breach of trust and people telling your business by who you expose yourself to.

You can't control jealousy, rumors or gossip, but you can limit betrayal, breach of trust and people telling your business by who you expose yourself to. #Ap2w

Don't make a habit of giving people the benefit of the doubt. Somebody always wants something that you have. The scary part is not knowing the somebody. Trust is earned, not given.

A true test of one's character is the ability to forgive those who betray you, overlook those who look down on you, turn the other cheek to those who try to take advantage of you, look in the face of those who talk about you behind your back, make up with those who have never said they were sorry, coexist with those who you know can't be trusted, talk around those who you know are looking for something to repeat, do something for those who you know wouldn't do the same for you, wish happiness upon those who want nothing but bad for you and pray for those who you know would never pray for you.

Don't expect a poisonous snake to transition into a pet kitten. Sometimes the good in us wants to give others the benefit of the doubt when they've done nothing to deserve it. Expecting someone to be something they've never been will generally leave you feeling hurt, disappointed or betrayed. Trust what you actually see and not what you envision.

Don't ever blame someone for betraying your trust when they did nothing to earn it. #Ap2w

If you have to wonder if they're truly in your corner, they're probably not. If you have to wonder if you can truly trust them, you probably can't, and if you have to question if they truly have your best interest at heart, they probably don't. It's not loyalty if you have to question it.

A L W A Y S

Don't ever allow anyone to take you for granted. Always think, believe and act as if you're relevant.

Humility will always open more doors and create more opportunity than pride or self-pity. #Ap2w

#Ap2w

I was cleaning out my closet yesterday and realized how much it relates to our lives. Some things hold memories, and even though we don't wear them much anymore we will always cherish and hold on to them. Some things are from a different era in our lives, and even though they may be nice items, we can pass them on because they are now out of style to us. Some things we've simply outgrown, and they need to be discarded. If we never make room for new things in our closet and try to hold on to everything from our past, then we eventually end up standing still because we run out of space to grow.

Always be an example of what's right. You cannot pretend to be something that you don't live. #Ap2w

Oftentimes we hope and wish for change, when in reality our current situation is a clear sign that it's us who need to make changes, but we're too blinded by our own egos to see it. Humility will always open more doors and create more opportunity than pride or self-pity.

Always refrain from demonstrating behavior or characteristics you don't like to see present in others. If you don't like snitches, don't be a snitch; if you don't like gossipers, don't gossip; if you don't like arrogance, demonstrate humility; if you don't like liars, don't be a liar; if you don't like users, don't be a user; and if you don't like ungratefulness, always show gratitude.

#Ap2w

The more prepared you are, the less you have to depend on luck.

There's not a day I wake up that my mind is not on how to do something differently, cleverer or simply better than my competition. Competition is not only restricted to other teams or coaches, but also is relevant to every aspect of my life. Someone is always looking to outdo or replace you if you have anything worth having. No matter how hard you've worked, what you've provided or given, the moment you become complacent is the moment you allow the competition to close the gap.

RESPECT

As we grow, we also evolve. Personal change will cause you to leave some things and people behind. They may not always like or understand your choices, but give them no choice but to respect them.

You don't have to impress, please or prove anything to those who truly respect you. #Ap2w

A person who does not understand, encourage or respect your dreams, goals or aspirations can only stop, limit or hold you back from obtaining them. Sometimes you simply have to leave people behind in order to move forward.

#Ap2w

Don't give others the power to tear down what you've worked so hard to build up. There will always be someone who doesn't respect you, your time, your space, your relationship, your household or your life the same way that you do. Instead of entertaining them, simply keep them at a distance and ignore their negativity. Happiness and peace of mind are far too hard to come by to put in the hands of someone who dwells in misery.

If you spend your time worrying about those who don't like, respect or agree with you, you will never have time or sanity for much else. #Ap2w

Whether you're a man or a woman, if you have to constantly ask, beg or teach a person how to treat you, how to respect you, how to pay attention to you or how to make time for you, no matter how much time, money or effort you've invested and as painful as it may be to accept, that person is not the one for you. Although no relationship is perfect, some things should simply come natural.

I've never concerned myself with wanting anyone to admire me for what I have. I've always lived so that people respect me for who I am.

You shouldn't have to educate people who truly care about you on how to treat or respect you.

There's always going to be someone who doesn't agree with, like or respect you. If you spend all of your time worrying about or concerning yourself with them, you'll never have much time for anything else. If someone has a problem with you, let it be their problem not yours.

COMPLAINING

Feeling sorry for yourself will never solve your problems, and others only feel sorry for you for so long. Everyone has something they can complain about; some just realize better than others how much of a waste of time it is.

Anyone can find something to complain about if you choose to. It's all in your attitude. Count your blessings, not your misfortunes. #Ap2w

I've failed just as much as I've succeeded, but you'd never know because I've never slowed down to complain. I've come up short just as many times as I've come out on top, but it's invisible to you because all you see is me pushing forward. I listen just as much as I talk because I realize once you stop listening you stop learning. I'm a step ahead even when it may seem as though I'm a step behind because I always play to win.

You can complain about the things you don't have or express pride about the things you do. You can dwell on the negative events that took place yesterday or look forward to the positive opportunities that tomorrow presents. You can make excuses as to why you can't do things or you can make up your mind to find a way to get things done. It's all in your attitude.

I've failed just as much as I've succeeded, but you'd never know because I've never slowed down to complain. #Ap2w

Everyone has problems, misfortunes or complaints they could share, but if you're reading this your blessing is better than some who are no longer here to read, write or speak. Even a bad day or your worst day is a good day because it's the blessing of another day.

You can be depressed or in the dumps about the negative things in your life or thankful and proud of the positive things in your life. It all depends on the attitude you have about life. We can all find something to complain about or something to be grateful for. The choice is yours.

Some people complain about their problems, some want or expect others to feel sorry for them about their problems, some blame others for their problems, some ignore their problems, some weigh their blessings against their problems, some search for solutions to their problems, and some choose to pray about their problems. Your attitude about anything you're faced with in life is your choice.

#Ap2w

You can complain about your lack of assets, sources or ability, or you can find a way to balance it out. It's all in your attitude. I'm not as talented as a lot of people in a lot of areas, but I make a habit of doing the little things better than everyone else.

No matter what the nature of the relationship, make a habit of surrounding yourself with people who are healthy for you. If you don't, you'll always have people problems and complaints.

We all have problems at some point or another in life. What separates us is how we choose to face or deal with them. #Ap2w

If you spend more time crying than laughing, complaining than appreciating, frowning than smiling, or making up than making memories, you're probably with the wrong person.

If your attitude, mood or outlook is negative, then your days, weeks and months are probably going to be the same. It's no accident that positive people are generally happy and negative people are not. Anyone can find something to frown, complain or be bitter about. It's your choice whether or not you allow it to control you.

F R I E N D

A friend should be an asset, not a liability. Reevaluate anyone that fits into the liability category.

You don't have to purchase something for someone in order to give them something. Simply being trustworthy, supportive, encouraging, positive and not being a burden is a blessing. It's called friendship.

A true friend generally offers or gives much more than they expect in return. A user generally does the opposite. #Ap2w

There is a huge difference between responsibilities and choices. We often get so caught up in what we've made our priorities that we lose sight of what *should* be our priorities. For example, a child is a responsibility and a relationship is a choice. If a personal relationship, family relationship or friendship strains, drains, stresses or depresses you, there's always a choice to separate or distance yourself from it. No one controls where you devote your time and attention, but you.

Knowing when to state your opinion and when to keep it to yourself is very important in life. Not knowing this can and will cost you opportunities, friends, family and much more. Regardless of how strongly you may feel, some things are simply better left unsaid.

#Ap2w

It's sad but true that some of the people you extend your hand to help out in life only have the intention to pull you down. Choose your friends wisely. Trust is earned, not given.

There's someone in each of our lives who a lot of others would love to have that we take for granted. There's someone who supports each of us through thick and thin that we give little or no attention to in return. There's someone who considers themself a true friend to each of us that we treat like a mere associate. There's someone who loves each of us unconditionally that we only express or show our love to under certain circumstances or conditions. Special people are hard to come by in life. Don't ever take that for granted. A dead person can't smell flowers.

Whether it's a friendship, relationship or business, don't entertain people who have the potential and consistently threaten to let you down, betray your trust or break your heart. The reward is not worth the risk, and there are enough genuine people out there who are less of a gamble.

Whether it's a friend, companion or organization, never blame yourself for someone not seeing the good in you. No matter how much it's worth, how many bidders there are for it or how rare it may be, some people will simply never recognize the beauty or value in the most exclusive works of art.

She's there to praise you in your proudest moments and to support you in your darkest hours. She forgives you for the things you've done and doesn't judge you for the things you've neglected to do. She understands when no one else understands, and she cares when no one else seems to care. She's an advisor when you need advice and provides a listening ear when you need to talk. She loves you just the same no matter what you do or say. She's been a constant source of stability when others have walked away. She was there at the very beginning, and she will be there until the end. She's your rock and your foundation. She's your very best friend. If you're lucky enough to have her, make sure you cherish her. She's your Mom.

Be careful not to lose your true friends trying to entertain and make new friends.

Real friends don't betray you, try to compete with you, talk about you, wish for you to fail, search for dirt on you, try to expose you or feel jealous towards you. They encourage you, support you, protect you, endorse you and defend you against others. Some of the people who claim the most loyalty towards you are, in fact, the most disloyal to you.

You should never have to question who your true friends are. #Ap2w

Just because someone has done something for you in the past doesn't mean you owe them for the rest of your life.

#Ap2w

Far too often people expect something in return for what should have been normal gestures of friendship or family love. Just because you may have helped me along the way doesn't mean I'm obligated to carry you the rest of the way.

The more people you tell your personal business to the less personal your business becomes. Always remember that every close friend of yours has a close friend of theirs that they share information with who's not that close to you.

Always be aware of those who act extra or go above and beyond to prove their loyalty or friendship. What's real does not have to be dressed up or accessorized.

If you only communicate with people when you want or need something they have, you appear to them just like everyone else who only communicates with them when they want or need something they have. Networking, communication and friendship should be an all-the-time thing.

Everyone wants to claim friendship, but very few are willing to pledge loyalty. #Ap2w

Insecure or jealous friends are future *former* friends. Don't cry over those you've left behind. They are where they wanted or deserve to be.

Whether it's friends, associates or family, if you can't trust those in your circle, you need to either remove yourself or them from it. Very rarely do our instincts lie to us when it comes to who we can or cannot trust. It's a matter of whether or not we choose to listen.

Popularity is overrated. It's not about how many friends you have, it's about how many of the right kind of friends you have. The bigger the circle, the greater the chances of betrayal, deceit, jealousy, gossip and slander. It's that simple. Keep your circle small and keep prayer constant.

It's not about how many friends you have, it's about how many of the right kind of friends you have. #Ap2w

If you are a good person, then you will often be a better friend to others than they are to you. Don't ever get discouraged by this because there's nothing bad about being genuine or having a good heart.

Beware of people who are never at fault. They always have an excuse and rarely accept responsibility, which makes them hard to trust. Whether it's a friend, family or significant other, an unaccountable companion is a dangerous companion.

If you're fortunate enough to have someone that you consider a true friend, don't take it for granted because they're rare and hard to find. Take a moment to let those who are loyal to you know how much you appreciate them.

#Ap2w

CONFIDENCE

Never give anyone the power to control your confidence, moods or state of mind with rumors or gossip. People are going to talk as long as this world keeps spinning, so don't let it stop you from living.

Work on **you** today. You have your faults, imperfections, attitude, personality, self-esteem, confidence, relationship, parenting skills, being a friend and so much more that you can focus on. If you commit to it, there shouldn't be much time left to concern yourself with anyone else.

Confidence is all about attitude. #Ap2w

I'm confident because I know what I'm willing to do to avoid failure. I'm proud because I know what I've sacrificed to get to where I am. I'm driven because I know nothing in life stays the same. I don't brag because arrogance is an unattractive trait. I'm not lazy because I'm ambitious. I'm humble because my mother taught me the importance of humility. I'm cautious about what I say or do because I respect those I represent. I'm generous because I believe my blessings come as a result of blessing others. I'm responsible because I have others depending on me. I have peace of mind because I don't worry about things I can't control. I'm not jealous because I'm grateful. I don't have confrontations because I mind my own business. I don't dwell on my problems because it's not going to solve them.

I don't complain because I'd sound like those I don't like to listen to. I don't feel sorry for myself because life and this world don't feel sorry for me. I'm happy because life is too short to be sad. I will never lose because I will always play to win! This is a portrait of who I am.

Arrogance is behavior. It can be very misleading. Confidence is a state of mind. It's who you are despite who's watching. There is a difference. #Ap2w

My pride would never allow me to talk down on someone else to lift my own position, and my confidence would never allow me to be jealous of or upset with someone else's position. My humility would never allow me to brag about my personal accomplishments, and my personality would never allow me to expose or tell someone else's business. My loyalty would never allow me to breach a bond of trust, and there's nothing that could make me betray a true friend's trust.

Confidence is all about attitude. I never fail; I just sometimes come up short. I'm never behind; I just haven't caught up yet. I didn't get rejected; they just picked the wrong person. I wasn't wrong; I just made a mistake. I'm good enough; I just haven't reached my full potential. I can do it; I just haven't learned how to yet. I will succeed because failure is not an option.

I don't think I'm any better than anyone else; I just have certain standards I've set for myself. I'm not stuck up; I just refuse to entertain drama. I'm not arrogant; I just have a very high level of confidence. I'm not impatient; I just don't have a tolerance for nonsense. I'm not unfriendly; I just have no interest in dealing with fake people. I'm not talking to or about anyone in particular; I'm just giving a description of who I am.

A man who's not strong, secure or confident *before* he has anything does not suddenly gain those characteristics because he does. Money, popularity, material things or possessions only expose your weaknesses to those who can see past what most admire about you. True self-confidence should exist no matter where you work, what you have or what you do. It's just who you are.

Confidence attracts admirers and creates haters at the same time. You can't control which side of the fence your observers land on, so don't worry or try. Just be you. #Ap2w

If you are truly confident in who you are, what you stand for and what you're about, you should never be affected by negative comments, criticism or analogies. There's always going to be someone looking to talk down on you or bring you down. As long as you're pleasing in the eyes of God, nothing else really matters.

#Ap2w

WISDOM

Be humble in victory and be humble in defeat because neither last for long.

Oftentimes you can't control getting knocked down, but don't ever give anyone the satisfaction of watching you stay down.

It's not about the size of the mountain, it's about the ambition of the climber. #Ap2w

Don't ever allow yourself to become complacent. Elite performers elevate their skill level by elevating their preparation.

Good leaders don't have to ask people to follow them. Their leadership and productivity makes people want to follow them.

We are known for the popular things that we do in life, but we are remembered for the impactful things that we have done. Be known or be remembered.

There's no point in arguing, responding or reacting to any-one who says things about you on social media. It's smarter and much easier to just block them. Don't ever give anyone who doesn't behave like they're on your level the power to pull you to their level.

#Ap2w

Don't expect sympathy for crying the same sad song over and over because people only feel sorry for you for so long in life, if at all. If you don't like what you're getting, you may need to change what you're doing.

It's okay to give a gift or a blessing, but it's much more important to be considered the gift and the blessing.

If you always sit around and wait on others to give you something, then you will never have much of anything for yourself.

A simple recipe for peace of mind is to separate yourself from distractions or remove them from your life.

Drama is generally one person's jealousy, messiness or misery until it's entertained by others. Then it spreads. Don't give dramatic people the satisfaction of fueling their flames.

Live life while you still have life because you don't get a replay. #Ap2w

If someone knocks you down, don't you dare give them the satisfaction of seeing you stay down.

I wasn't a straight A student and my conduct report wasn't squeaky clean, but I was smart enough to look up to and surround myself with people who were in positions I wanted to be in. I wanted to break the track records of my big brother, Darius Jones, so I was motivated to work extra hard to be as good as I could be. The first time I saw Tony Rice play college football on TV as a small town kid, I made up my mind I was going to duplicate that. The first time I saw JJ Dawkins wearing a Phi Beta Sigma Fraternity jacket, I knew I wanted one for myself. And when I met my college teammate, Deano Orr, I admired him for his intelligence in addition to his athletic ability, and I knew I wanted to be viewed the same way. We all are a product of those we've at one time followed; therefore, teach and encourage young people to follow individuals who are leading them in the right direction.

When you stoop to someone else's level, you put yourself on their level. #Ap2w

Don't waste your time waiting on someone to change. Despite how much you may have invested, you can't force others to be what they have not committed themselves to being.

Holding a grudge generally affects you far worse than it affects the individuals you hold it against. Life is too short to give anyone the power to affect your moods and emotions over an extended period of time. Unless someone has violated you physically or committed a personal crime against you, it's probably much easier to forgive and move on than store resentment or hatred toward them.

#Ap2w

It's okay to be criticized, corrected or critiqued. Individuals who think they know everything learn nothing.

You don't reach the top of a mountain by accident. It takes preparation, hard work, determination and sacrifice. Wishful thinking or depending on luck will only keep you at the bottom of the hill looking up. #Ap2w

Sometimes trying to be what everyone else wants or needs you to be for them can cause you to lose touch with yourself. When you're being pulled in multiple directions, you have to step back, take a deep breath and take time to take care of yourself. You can't take care of others if you neglect to take care of yourself. There's no harm in catering to you.

It doesn't matter who believes in us as long as we believe in us.

You should never have to explain or prove to others how genuine or sincere you are. It should always show.

No matter what you do, never become complacent. Someone is always waiting on you to slip up so they can slide in.

Don't measure your success by assets, dollars and cents. Measure your success by happiness, peace of mind and lack of regrets.

As men, black or white, we can't argue against anything that our actions or reactions mimic. Like it or not, stereotypes exist because we constantly fuel them.

The best cleanse you can do for your mind, body and soul is to rid yourself of the people who act as toxins that affect your overall health and peace of mind. Some individuals simply need to be flushed out of your life.

Trying to please everyone only prevents you from being true to who you really are. #Ap2w

One act of violence doesn't solve another. It only creates more chaos. We should seek solutions, not vengeance. All lives matter.

Adult dependency more often than not results in disappointment. It always has, and it always will. The only way to ensure that something is going to get done is to do it yourself.

It's easy to join in on the rumors, gossip or negative conversation about others until it's about you or someone close to you. We all have enough skeletons in our closet, history we're not proud of and acts that have never come to light in our own lives, so we have no place to judge or concern ourselves with the lives of others.

It's never our place to question an act of God. If you don't believe this, you will forever struggle coming to terms with His will.

People may knock you down or off track, but the only person that controls whether or not you get back up is you. Don't ever give another person the power to keep you down.

If you're tired of the cards that life keeps dealing out, you may need to change the deck that you're playing with. #Ap2w

Don't depend on people who have done nothing to earn credibility just because you think they should act a certain way towards you. Doing so only sets you up for disappointment.

Place your stock in people who show you more than they tell you.

No matter what a person buys, gives or provides you with, time is the most valuable thing they can give you. If a person is not giving you their time, they are simply buying themselves time. If a person is giving you their time, don't take it for granted; make the most of it.

Just because you have a good heart doesn't give anyone the right to take advantage of it.

#Ap2w

When you have something to lose, there's always going to be someone with nothing to lose looking to bring you down. Make wise choices and decisions.

Instead of trying to be like someone else, I always set my sights on being unlike anyone else. #Ap2w

No matter how many days it rains, the sun is sure to always shine again. You just have to be mentally tough enough to weather the storm.

The best way to maintain peace of mind is to refrain from worrying about things that you cannot control.

Regardless of how much you have invested, don't ever second guess ridding yourself of something or someone that's become a distraction. No matter what you're doing or where you're trying to go, the less weight you have to carry the easier it is to climb.

One of the perks of life that many often forget is we control who and what we let affect us. #Ap2w

Judge how valuable you are to a person not by what they give you they have an abundance of, but by how much of the things they don't have much of that they share with you.

#Ap2w

No matter what you had going on yesterday, today is a new day. When tomorrow comes, this day will be gone and you will never get it back. Don't waste it dwelling on or trying to change yesterday because you can't. Make today count.

Never fall for a nice body or a handsome or pretty face without knowing what comes with it. Physical attraction will generally cost you far more than it benefits you if that's all you're working with.

Time is one of the most valuable assets we have. Don't waste it or take it for granted. #Ap2w

Age, success, finances or lack of doesn't classify you as a man. Being able to look in the mirror at your reflection and know that you act, conduct and carry yourself as one makes you a man.

Don't measure your success by how much money you do or don't have. Measure it by how much regret you do or don't have.

Don't ever give anyone the power to make you act out of character. You will be judged on your actions and reactions, regardless of who provoked them. You will never go wrong being the bigger person.

Don't tell it if you don't want it repeated.

#Ap2w

Social media is good for networking, staying in touch, reconnecting and sharing photos. It's not a place to have public arguments, air out dirty laundry or discuss private issues. If you don't have respect for the other party or parties involved, at least have respect for yourself.

You can send flowers, give gifts, buy toys or say nice things, but never take for granted that the most important thing you can give to anyone you care about is your time.

Regardless of how much you know or think you know, a person who isn't willing to listen is a person who doesn't want to learn.

It's usually not an accident if bad things continue to happen to you. If you don't like what you're getting, then change what you're doing.

Don't ever try to fit in just to be liked or accepted. The more common you are, the more unoriginal you are. #Ap2w

You can appear to have everything on the surface, but if you're not at peace with yourself and don't like the image that you see in the mirror when no one else is looking, you have nothing.

Why beg someone for something that someone else is willing and able to offer you?

#Ap2w

Doing the right thing can cause you to be bored, lonely and even considered lame, but it's a sacrifice most have to make for success.

Jealousy, dislike, resentment or hatred will always affect the other party more than it does you unless you personally allow it to affect you.

If you learn to stand alone before you become dependent on someone else, you will always be able to stand on your own with or without their support.

It's hard to be lazy and successful at anything. The two simply don't go hand-in-hand. #Ap2w

Count your blessings and not your misfortunes. No matter how bad you think you have it, there's always someone who has it a lot worse.

In order to determine if anyone meets your standards, you must first set standards for yourself.

My mother always told me that the worst reputation you can have is to be a person who wants or needs something every time you come around.

Never make kids promises that you can't keep. They rely on and take to heart your every word.

#Ap2w

There's always going to be someone who doesn't want to see you succeed; therefore, keep your circle small and your business private.

If you are good to others, good things will happen to and for you. #Ap2w

Jealousy and insecurity are characteristics that will constantly cause people to behave in ways that reflect badly on or embarrass themselves.

You get questions answered by asking questions. You obtain your goals by striving for them. You get what you want by going to get it. You fulfill your dreams by waking up and acting on them. In order to finish you must start. Don't ever be left saying, "What if," "I should have," "Why didn't I," "I wish I had" or "I intended to."

We often hold ourselves back by waiting on someone else to open the door of opportunity for us. #Ap2w

Make the most of every day that you have, because your future as far as you know could be shorter than your past.

Even though you may feel as if they can do it, every time you ask someone for a favor take into consideration how many others have asked them for the same or a similar favor before you.

#Ap2w

You get what you want by going to get it. You fulfill your dreams by waking up and acting on them. In order to finish you must start. #Ap2w

No one is perfect, but we can usually balance things out with honesty and sincerity.

You may not be able to change a negative stereotype, but you can control whether or not you contribute to the reason that it exists.

Anything you do with passion generally has a domino effect. It simply has a way of motivating and affecting those around you. #Ap2w

You can't prop someone's eyes open and hope that they will see the good in you. Eventually blindness will set in no matter how much time or effort you put into it. If you often find yourself trying to prove points, you're simply dealing with the wrong person.

#Ap2w

MESSAGE TO MY DAUGHTERS

I talk to my daughters openly about everything because far too many fathers fail to or are uncomfortable doing so. I don't want them to hear or see something for the first time and not know how to act or react to it. As a man, I know how men think, what they do, what their expectations and intentions are; therefore I try to educate, advise and prepare them in advance. I'm not saying they will always listen because we all have to go through things for ourselves in order to grow, but it won't be from lack of knowledge. When they fall, I'm not there to say, "I told you so." I'm there to say, "This is why I tried to tell you so," and to help them get back on their feet. There will never be too many messages to my daughters.

Refuse to settle. #Ap2w

Classy is not the new sexy. Classy is what far too many of the new generations fail to understand.

Don't ever let there be a difference in your value and your price. You can't make a man treat you right or respect you, but you do determine if he's given the opportunity to mistreat or disrespect you. If you set the bar high, it will generally weed out those not willing to or capable of understanding your worth and high standards. Refuse to settle.

#Ap2w

A successful man is generally not interested in a woman who he knows he has to carry because she simply wants to share his world. He's interested in carrying and sharing his world with a woman who he knows is very capable and willing to carry herself.

Don't expect anyone to respect your standards if you never set any for yourself. #Ap2w

Don't expect a man to show you any more respect than you demonstrate for yourself. If you present yourself as easy, he's going to take you for being easy. If you present yourself in a non-classy manner, he's not going to treat you as if you have class. If you act as if you're money hungry, he's going to look at you as if you're all about money. If you always like to party, he's going to look at you only as a party girl. And if you never stand up for yourself, always appear as needy or weak, he's always going to think of and treat you as such.

Don't expect a man to have long term intentions for you if you act as if you don't have long term expectations for yourself. If you give yourself to him quickly or easily, then he's not going to look at it as if he's special. He's going to look at you as if you are not. If you do everything for him without him giving you much in return, then he's going to assume that's a pattern of yours as opposed to a perk of his. Men like and sometimes even love what's fun, easy, spontaneous and comes with little or no obligations.

#Ap2w

However, men marry what takes time, effort, work, responsibility and demands respect.

If you have to constantly instruct a man on how to treat you, remind him of the things that are important to you, persuade him to compliment you, convince him to pay attention to you, ask him to tell you how he feels about you, beg him to spend time with you or wonder if he really cares about you, he's probably not the one for you.

Men like and sometimes even love what's fun, easy, spontaneous and comes with little or no obligations. However, men marry what takes time, effort, work, responsibility and demands respect. #Ap2w

Despite what you may see on reality TV, there is nothing attractive or appealing about a grown woman fighting. Always carry yourself as if you are or will one day be someone's mother.

One of the best compliments you can receive as a woman is that you have class. One of the worst insults you can receive is that you don't have any.

If all you have to offer someone are good looks and an appealing body, then you will forever be on borrowed time. You'll always be one step away from another pretty face or sexy walk taking your place.

#Ap2w

Don't ever be so ashamed or embarrassed at what others will think of your failed relationships that you stay in them and endure disrespect, mistreatment or abuse of any kind. Regardless of how frustrating or disappointing it may be to start over, there's no quota on being fair to yourself.

Don't dress to get a man's attention. Present and carry yourself in a way that captures his imagination. #Ap2w

The way a woman presents herself is a direct reflection of her character. While every woman has the right to possess an inner alter ego, it is not always ideal for the outside world to see. The way you dress often determines the type of man you're going to attract or what type of intentions he's going to have for you.

Always remember: no matter how much attention it gets you, the more of your body you show, the less a man is going to be curious to see. What makes you valuable temporarily generally devalues you long term.

Although clubbing and going out is fun, keep in mind that established men don't search for girlfriends and wives in night clubs. They search for someone who likes to go out and have fun. What's popular in the world of nightlife is generally not what men bring to light. If you're interested in a certain type of guy, put yourself in the type of climate or environment where he's going to see and respect you.

Guys don't generally marry the fun chicks. They simply play with them until another toy steals their attention.

Who men stare at, wink at, whistle at, chase down, buy a drink for and even offer money to are not necessarily who they have long term intentions for. What they can't see, have to wonder about, need a certain approach for and can't buy is what not only grasps them, but keeps their attention.

Men are naturally observant of the things you pay attention to. If you're into money and material things, then that's what he's going to use to get and keep your attention, but keep in mind that he's generally not going to give you anything or do anything for you that he can't afford. He does what he needs to do in order to get what he wants.

The way you dress often determines the type of man you're going to attract or what type of intentions he's going to have for you. #Ap2w

An independent man is attracted to independence in a woman because he ultimately wants to know that her intentions for him are genuine. He knows his financial value and potential, but he also wants to know that's not the only thing she values about him.

Don't expect a man to treat you like, present you as or make you his queen if you don't carry or present yourself as one.

#Ap2w

You can't be like everyone else if you want what few of them have. The less someone can tell a man about you, the more interested he will be in making a commitment to you. What sets you apart is what makes you special and rare. It's wise to be different.

The more time you spend trying to get someone to treat you right, the less time you have to allow someone else to show you they already know how to do so. #Ap2w

No matter what he does, what he has or how popular he may be, a man needs and desires the attention of a woman over all else. By nature he knows how he should talk to a woman, by nature he knows he shouldn't put his hands on a woman, by nature he knows he should respect a woman, by nature he knows what it takes to get the attention of a woman and what it takes to keep it. If he's not giving his attention to you, then he's giving it to someone. If he's not spending time with you, then he's spending it with someone. If he's putting his hands on you, then there's somebody he wouldn't dare touch in a disrespectful way. If he's not treating you right, then he's treating someone right. The results you get as a woman are a direct result of the standards you set for yourself and the behavior you tolerate or allow from a man. There are no special exceptions, so don't try to convince yourself of this in order to keep the peace or give him time to get it right.

Every woman who you share the good or bad qualities about your man with is one you've potentially created curiosity, motivation or a challenge inside. No matter how close you are to your girlfriends, there are just certain things you should keep to yourself about your relationship with your man. Your friends may not be as loyal to you as you are to them. Every friend you have has a friend who is neither loyal to nor cares about you at all.

No matter what a man buys you, provides for you or does for you, the most valuable thing he can ever give to you is his time. Assets minus presence equal emptiness.

The more of a secret you are, the more of a commodity you will always be. #Ap2w

If you always base your happiness on or place it in the hands of someone else, then you'll never have control of it your-self. Happiness starts within. If you truly love who you are, then you will view yourself as an asset and never allow any-one to make you feel as if you're a liability. When you know and believe what you bring to the table, you quickly realize, regardless of the nature of the relationship, that everyone you meet or get involved with may not deserve you.

You should never have to try and make a man respect you, question why a man doesn't treat you right or ask a man if he really cares about you.

#Ap2w

Men are drawn to attractive females. Men are captivated by intelligent, attractive females. Men are captured by independent, intelligent, attractive females. If you can stand alone, then he will be much quicker to volunteer to carry you than if he feels as if he has to carry you because you can't or don't want to carry yourself. Needy or greedy females are a turnoff to guys who are attracted to independence.

Always keep an open and unselfish heart. Something that means little or nothing to you could mean the world to someone else. I firmly believe that our blessings stem from blessing others. #Ap2w

The quickest way to run a man off is to nag him or become a distraction because you're insecure or acting jealous. If he gives you a reason to doubt him, you should already know where you stand. If he doesn't, then don't create one because of what the last guy did.

Be careful who you do things around, say things around, or tell your personal business to. People who are always in other people's business will quickly spread your business.

Regardless of how close you may think you are, the more females you tell your relationship business to the more criticism and competition you create for yourself. Some things should simply remain between you and him.

#Ap2w

A man who initially caters to you, respects you, gives you his time, showers you with attention and makes you a priority wants to conquer you. A man who consistently does all of these things wants to capture and keep you. You should never have to question your worth to a man who truly values you.

If a man leaves you for respecting yourself and demanding his, then he was never yours or had any intentions to be.

Don't ever feel as if you have to fit in to be accepted. People don't have to like you to respect you.

Don't ever allow a man to treat you any differently than your father treats you. Set standards for yourself and demand that he meets them. You are a diamond; make sure he treats you as such.

If a man truly loves, respects and honors you, then every day should feel like Valentine's Day. #Ap2w

The more you tell others about your relationship, the more you involve outsiders in your personal business. Everyone around you is not happy that you're happy. A few people around you are curious as to why you're so happy, and someone is outright jealous that you're happy. Sometimes a smile is enough to shine so keep the details to yourself.

#Ap2w

If you don't set standards for yourself and uphold them, don't expect a man to respect them. A man can only do what you allow him to. The price of having standards or being a good woman is often loneliness, but it's a better alternative than knowingly wasting your time on someone who has nothing but physical or short term intentions for you.

Don't ever get involved with someone you feel you will have to change in order to be happy. #Ap2w

If you are truly something special, you may suffer heartache countless times before you find someone who truly appreciates your worth and what you stand for because it takes a very rare individual to appreciate one. Not many will be worthy of you. Many may hurt, betray or disappoint you. There's no time or age limit on finding a good man; therefore, no matter how many times you come up short, always stay true to who and what you are.

Be careful who you seek or take relationship advice from. You never know who wants what you have because they don't have it themselves.

You should never have to talk someone into respecting or treating you right. If you spend most of your time wondering, wishing and wanting, then you're probably wasting your time.

#Ap2w

Being a woman with standards will often result in frustration or unhappiness because it will often leave you unfulfilled and lonely. Men generally have multiple options because so many women give into this and as a result are willing to lower their standards and settle for less than they deserve. Always remember that if you allow a man to test drive your product at will, he won't ever have motivation or a reason to fully buy in. You have the power to control how you're treated. Whether or not you exercise your power or settle is your choice.

The type of man you attract is usually a direct reflection of what attracted him to you. If it was your appealing character, vibrant personality, intelligent conversation or classy sex appeal, then he will treat you as such. If it was your seductive attire, provocative dancing, revealing photos or intoxicated actions, then that's how he's going to always view and treat you. There are few exceptions. You catch the type of fish that's attracted to the bait you're using.

You catch the type of fish that's attracted to the bait you're using. #Ap2w

Regardless of how mean, insensitive, inattentive, rude or unaffectionate a man may seem, every man treats some-one right. Don't ever ignore obvious signs. When the way he treats you changes, the way he views and feels about you has probably changed also.

#Ap2w

If you find yourself complaining, disappointed or crying more than you're surprised, satisfied or smiling, then you're probably with the wrong person. Good men do exist. You just have to make up your mind that you're not going to settle for a bad one just to say you have one.

You should never have to question your worth to a man who truly values you. #Ap2w

You have the power to control how you're treated. Whether or not you exercise your power or settle is your choice.

Don't ever get involved with someone you feel you will have to change in order to be happy. It's one thing to grow with someone who is wanting and willing to grow with you, but it's another thing altogether to feel you can change who they truly are. Users don't all of a sudden become caretakers. Abusers don't all of a sudden become protectors. And disrespectful guys do not all of a sudden become respectful men.

No matter how much time you invest in a man, how much energy you put into him, how much benefit of the doubt you give him, how much faith you have in him, how much potential you see in him or how many times you forgive him, you will never turn a donkey into a thoroughbred or stallion. No matter how powerful or influential you think you are, sometimes you have to accept what you see and cut your losses.

#Ap2w

I'm happy because life is too short to be sad. I will never lose because I will always play to win! This is a portrait of who I am.

#Ap2w

TRIBUTE

Some people enter your life and have a lasting impact on you. I was taught by Mrs. Kaye Simmons in 5th grade in 1984. She saw something in me that I didn't see in myself at that point in life and challenged me to be elite in every aspect of my life. She was more than just a teacher to me; she was an Angel. Her voice and words of wisdom have influenced me throughout my life. I witnessed her fight a 5 year battle with cancer with an admirable amount of courage and strength. Her fight was the inspiration for numerous quotes in this book. Even though she is no longer with us, she will forever encourage me to **Always Play To Win.** Proceeds from #Ap2w will establish a Kaye Summer Simmons scholarship in honor of her.

IN LOVING MEMORY
Mrs. Kaye Summer Simmons
November 20, 1947 - June 3, 2017

Reactions to Derek's Quotes on Facebook:

"There aren't words to express my thanks to Derek Jones, and how he supported my mama and my family. There really aren't words that seem adequate to explain the type of man he is. And, honestly, words are great, but his character and actions speak far more about him."
— Kerri Simmons McAlister

"Long overdue! I get so much from your quotes...now more people can benefit from them!"
— Princess Plummer Pedew

"I have been waiting on this book because your posts are great!"
— Nikita Hollingsworth Forest

"Fantastic DJ! I am looking forward to the read." **— Kevin Briggs**

"Amen! Your words were uplifting my spirits during my recuperation from my surgery. I really appreciate your inspiration!"
— Paul Jones

"You are an awesome writer." **— Sherry Browning Norman**

"Man, I love your inspiring words!" **— Tarsha Bethley Marshall**

"I was the guy that shot the cannon every time you scored a TD in high school. Thank you from the bottom of my heart for the heart felt things you said about my Kaye. I will never stop praying for you and your lovely family! As Coach Varner would say WIN! That's what we Wolverines do best!"
— Terry Simmons

"Men need this." **— Kimberly Bracket**

Made in the USA
Las Vegas, NV
18 December 2021

38465562R00063